STEAM IN THE COUNTRYSIDE

THE

1950s

From the footplate of No. 46200 *The Princess Royal* at Llandudno Junction. The Stanier Pacifics were seen on the North Wales coastal route from time to time. On this occasion the locomotive was on a special working for railway enthusiasts.

STEAM IN THE COUNTRYSIDE

THE

1950s

ERIC OLDHAM

ALAN SUTTON

First published in the United Kingdom in 1994
Alan Sutton Publishing Limited
Phoenix Mill · Far Thrupp · Stroud · Gloucestershire

British Library Cataloguing in Publication Data

A catalogue record for this book is available from the British Library

ISBN 0–7509–0556–5

Typeset in 10/12 Palatino.
Typesetting and origination by
Alan Sutton Publishing Limited.
Printed and bound in Great Britain by
WBC, Bridgend, Mid Glam.

CONTENTS

Acknowledgement

The author is indebted to the public relations and publicity departments of British Railways for lineside facilities in connection with this book.

INTRODUCTION

Images of steam form the photographic content of this book. They graphically illustrate the working railways of the 1950s and feature a wide variety of locomotives and rolling stock. The landscape of Britain forms the backcloth to all the scenes in this collection. It is here that the steam locomotive is seen in all its moods, expressing visual power and majesty. Who has not succumbed to the whistle down the wind, the pattern of sunlight and steam, and the sounds of the countryside?

The charm of the branch line and the exhilaration of main line traffic both have their place in this book, which records many days spent by the lineside in what may be described as steam's Indian summer.

The steam locomotives inherited by British Railways were quite remarkable. Many originated in the days of the former railway companies, both pre- and post-1923. Some ran throughout their lives on the lines for which they had been built. Added to these were the locomotives designed by British Railways itself which were destined to have a comparatively short life.

With the advent of diesel–electric and electrification projects in the late 1950s, the days of the steam locomotive were numbered and it was gradually phased out in the following decade. When the last steam passenger train ran on 11 August 1968, people in their thousands paid their respect on the Settle and Carlisle section of the former Midland Railway. On that historic day the sound of steam in the fells gave way to the sighing of the wind and the lonely call of the curlew – a worthy requiem indeed!

Steam in the Countryside

The

1950s

Stanier Pacific No. 46229 *Duchess of Hamilton* departs from Crewe with the 'Mid-day Scot' to Glasgow in 1959.

CHAPTER ONE

WEST COAST IMPRESSIONS – CREWE TO SHAP SUMMIT

The Cheshire countryside is illustrated in two sequences photographed on the outskirts of Crewe and Warrington. This is the county of dairy farming and agricultural produce, with its own distinctive landscape of rich pastureland. In both locations it will be noted that quadrupled tracks are a common feature, reflecting the density of traffic.

To the north of Preston the main line becomes double track. On leaving Carnforth, the landscape changes character and becomes mountainous. In the 30 miles to Shap Summit the line rises to 916 ft above sea level, with the last 4 miles on a gradient of 1 in 75, a veritable sting in the tail. With scattered remnants of trees, pruned and shaped by the wind, Shap Fell presents a wild and spectacular landscape. More farming country is evident in the Lune valley and on Shap Fell, but the accent is still on sheep rearing.

Most of the locomotives responsible for working the line were built at Crewe, but there have been infiltrations from other works, notably Derby and Horwich.

Rebuilt 'Scot' No. 46125 climbs through the Cheshire countryside to the south of Crewe with a Barrow–London express. The locomotive, *3rd Carabinier*, was originally named *Lancashire Witch* when built in 1927. As first built, these locomotives had a large parallel boiler and squat chimney. The last of the class, which numbered seventy engines, was built as a high-pressure locomotive, but was rebuilt to conventional design in 1935. All the locomotives were subsequently rebuilt with tapered boilers as illustrated.

A Birmingham–Manchester train races down Madeley Bank towards Crewe in the early fifties hauled by Midland Compound No. 41078. Early BR livery has been applied to the locomotive and most of the rolling stock. This locomotive was one of the class built by the London, Midland and Scottish Railway during the period between 1924 and 1932.

No. 46202 was built as an experimental turbine-driven machine in 1933. Adapted from the 'Princess Royal' design, it spent most of its life working Liverpool–London traffic. Here it is seen south of Crewe with the 5.25 p.m. Liverpool–London train in 1951. After rebuilding to conventional design in 1952, it was involved in the tragic accident at Harrow and Wealdstone and was subsequently withdrawn from service.

A London and North Western 'Super D' 0–8–0 goods locomotive approaches Crewe on the Down Slow line with a loose-coupled freight. These locomotives were in their element hauling trains of 800 tons or more on the line between Preston and London, and were a common sight on the West Coast main line.

A Manchester–North Wales express leaves Winwick Junction, amid typical Cheshire farmland. The hay has been cut as the Standard BR class 5 4–6–0 proceeds towards Warrington. These locomotives performed similar duties to the LMS Stanier class 5 mixed-traffic locomotive, on which the design was based, and the first examples appeared in 1951.

A Euston–Carlisle train passes Winwick hauled by the pioneer LMS No. 46200 *The Princess Royal*, which was built at Crewe in 1933. Most of the rolling stock is of LMS origin. *The Princess Royal* was the first Pacific to be built for the London, Midland and Scottish and was designed by Sir William Stanier some seventeen months after he left the Great Western to take up his new appointment.

In early spring weather a BR class 2 passenger locomotive propels an engineer's train towards Warrington. These 2–6–0 engines were well suited to branch-line duties with their 5 ft diameter driving wheels. Sixty-five of these locomotives were built between 1953 and 1956.

An express freight train makes rapid progress as it heads north behind Stanier Pacific No. 46201 *Princess Elizabeth* on the section of line between Warrington and Winwick Junction. With the onslaught of dieselization, many express steam locomotives finished their days on mundane duties such as this. This popular member of the Stanier Pacifics has fortunately been preserved.

The Keswick portion of the 'Lakes Express' from London Euston leaves Oxenholme behind Stanier Pacific No. 46245 *City of London*, which was built at Crewe in 1943. The train divided at Oxenholme and the main portion then worked to Windermere. This accounts for the smaller portion of the train leaving for Penrith, where a suitable locomotive would take the train over the branch to Keswick.

The Down 'Royal Scot' north of Carnforth in 1951 working wrong line because of engineering operations. The locomotive is No. 46220 *Coronation*, which was originally streamlined for working the 'Coronation Scot' of 1937. On 29 June 1937 this locomotive attained a speed of 114 mph on the outskirts of Crewe on a test run with the new train.

No. 46250 *City of Lichfield* traverses the Lune valley with a heavy Birmingham–Glasgow train, which in normal conditions would be taken unassisted over Shap. In the event of assistance being required for the climb, banking engines were provided at Tebay, and would be attached loosely coupled to the rear of the train.

The Down 'Midday Scot' enters the Lune valley as a storm gathers ahead. This train was usually entrusted to a Pacific, but on this occasion a 'Rebuilt Scot' had been substituted. The first coach is a through working from Plymouth to Glasgow and was attached at Crewe.

A Liverpool–Glasgow train enters the Lune gorge and makes a spirited passage behind 'Jubilee' class 4–6–0 No. 45703 *Thunderer*. Advantage would be taken to increase speed on this level stretch of line before the final climb to Shap Summit began in earnest.

Stanier 'Black 5' No. 45259 ambles through the pastoral Lune valley with a mixed freight during high summer. The hill in the background is known as Jeffrey's Mount. Beyond is Dillicar, where water troughs were situated shortly before the village and junction of Tebay.

The Lune valley in high summer. No. 46228 *Duchess of Rutland*, resplendent in red livery, is shown to advantage against this panorama of the countryside with a Birmingham–Glasgow train. The locomotive was built in 1938 and was originally streamlined and painted in maroon with gilt livery.

Looking south, one is rewarded with this superb view of the valley as it was before the coming of the motorway. Here, class 5 No. 45431 proceeds south on a parcels train. These mixed-traffic locomotives were a valuable asset being available for a wide range of duties.

Looking northwards towards Tebay we are confronted with this view of WD 'Austerity' 2–8–0 No. 90187. Built during the Second World War, it survived to be taken into BR stock. It is seen hauling a train of Shap granite.

'The Lakes Express' runs serenely through the valley on a summer evening hauled by class 5 4–6–0 No. 45083. A variety of passenger locomotives were used on this working but the use of a Stanier class 5 was unusual.

'Jubilee' class 4-6-0 No. 45654 *Hood* takes water from Tebay troughs en route from Liverpool to Glasgow. The opportunity was taken here to increase speed before the gruelling climb to Shap Summit.

Summer morning in the fells. 'Princess' class Pacific No. 46209 *Princess Beatrice* leaves Tebay troughs with milk empties for Appleby. Towards the end of their working lives, many express locomotives performed menial tasks as a result of dieselization.

Over the summit. Stanier Pacific No. 46225 *Duchess of Gloucester* begins a lively descent at Shap with the 'Midday Scot' to Euston. Exhilarating speeds were quickly attained on the 1 in 75 descending gradient to Tebay.

The Down 'Royal Scot' near Shap Summit on the notorious 1 in 75 gradient. Pacific No. 46253 *City of St Albans* makes steady progress with a train of thirteen vehicles.

'Jubilee' class 4–6–0 No. 45698 *Mars* begins the descent to Oxenholme as it traverses Shap Summit with a Glasgow–Liverpool train. Between 1934 and 1936, 191 of these locomotives were built. In LMS days all were painted in maroon livery, with the exception of No. 5552 *Silver Jubilee* which was named to commemorate the Silver Jubilee of King George V. This locomotive was finished in black with chrome fittings.

Early morning on Shap. Pacific No. 46220 *Coronation* raises the echoes as it nears the summit with a fitted freight for Carlisle. This locomotive, in company with many others, ended its days on secondary duties as the modernization plan of the late 1950s turned to other forms of motive power.

This is Shap Wells, situated a short distance south of the summit. Here, a Down express hauled by class 5 4–6–0 No. 45174 is assisted by a Fowler 2–6–4 tank locomotive at the rear.

'Jubilee' class No. 45643 *Rodney* makes steady progress on the 1 in 75 in the summer of 1951 with a Manchester–Glasgow train. This class of locomotive was a popular choice for these workings at that time.

The remote Shap Fell is shown to advantage in this panoramic view taken in the late fifties, as Pacific No. 46232 *Duchess of Montrose* brings the Birmingham–Glasgow train towards the summit. Shap Fell is a unique landscape fashioned over time, and is seen at its best on a day of sunshine and showers.

Unrebuilt 'Patriot' class 4–6–0 No. 45548 *Lytham St Annes* toils up the 1 in 75 in high summer with a train for the North. These three-cylinder locomotives were designed by Sir Henry Fowler and built at Derby between 1930 and 1933.

CHAPTER TWO

THE RAILWAY THAT DIED – THE WOODHEAD ROUTE

The former Great Central Railway from Manchester to Sheffield via Longdendale and Woodhead connected the two cities by crossing the Pennines. Heavy traffic from the Yorkshire and Derbyshire coalfields to the conurbations centred on Manchester and Liverpool formed the line's prime source of income. The coal trains were operated mainly by the Great Central Robinson 2–8–0s which first appeared in 1911, and these remained until the demise of steam. Passenger traffic on the route connected Manchester and Liverpool with the eastern counties, as well as Nottingham, Leicester and London Marylebone.

Work on the electrification of the route was commenced in the late 1930s by the London and North Eastern Railway but, with the advent of the Second World War, further progress was delayed until the end of hostilities in 1945. The electrification involved building a new double-track tunnel at Woodhead and this was completed in October 1953. In the following year, on 20 September, the railway between Manchester and Sheffield became Britain's first all-electric main line for the conveyance of both passengers and freight. In the 1970s, however, it was decided to close the line between Deepcar and Dinting because of a decline in traffic and the high cost of maintaining obsolete equipment, and the line finally faded into oblivion on 20 July 1981.

In the first year of nationalization the newly formed British Railways made tests with various locomotives as a prelude to new locomotive building. Here is the most unusual sight of Great Western 4–6–0 No. 6990 *Witherslack Hall* on the descent to Godley junction with a Marylebone–Manchester express.

After the war, the LNER introduced a large number of mixed-traffic locomotives to replace ageing locomotives which were due for withdrawal. Here, new B1 class 4–6–0 No. 1173, in its attractive apple-green livery, hauls a Glossop–Manchester train.

A Glossop to Manchester passenger train rounds the curve at Hattersley hauled by N5 0–6–2 No. 9353. This was a Manchester, Sheffield and Lincolnshire design and this particular locomotive dated from the turn of the century.

This is Britain's largest steam locomotive on test on the Manchester–Sheffield line in 1955. No. 69999 was an articulated Garratt locomotive, built in 1925 for banking duties in Yorkshire on the Wath–Penistone line. It is here seen after conversion to oil burning and was withdrawn later in the year.

A study of Dinting Viaduct near Glossop, with a train for Manchester leaving behind a Great Central 4–4–2 tank locomotive. The viaduct is 1455 ft long and carries the line 120 ft above Dinting Vale. When originally completed in 1844, it consisted of five timber arches, each of 125 ft span, and eleven brick approach arches of 50 ft span. It was subsequently rebuilt in the form in which we see it today.

The western portal of the notorious Woodhead Tunnel, built through solid rock, with its castellated ornamentation complete with gargoyles. The Up tunnel was opened in 1845, with the Down tunnel being ready for traffic in 1852. The Up tunnel suffered to some extent with ventilation problems, due to the small confines as well as the fact that the line was on a rising gradient of 1 in 201.

Class K3 2–6–0 No. 1963 approaches Torside in the last year of the London and North Eastern Railway, 1947. This picture is included as it captures the atmosphere of a windswept moorland landscape in early spring. The stone walling is a familiar feature of the area.

B1 No. 61312 heads a Manchester–London Marylebone express in the early years of nationalization. The vehicles are of LNER origin and were built to the design of Sir Nigel Gresley.

Here is the Harwich–Liverpool boat express racing down from Woodhead. B1 No. 1158 is in charge of this prestige working. Overhead equipment is now in place for the forthcoming electrical operation of the line.

A small farm holding in the Pennines struggles for a living in the bleak landscape as a Great Central 2–8–0 descends with a train of coal from Yorkshire. When coal was used for industrial and domestic purposes there was a day-long procession of such trains from the Yorkshire coalfields, with corresponding trains of empties returning in the opposite direction.

Spring in the Pennines B1 4–6–0 No. 61155 approaches Torside with the morning train to London. The second and third coaches are post-war vehicles painted in the early BR livery of carmine red and cream.

A Manchester–Sheffield train approaches Torside hauled by Co-Co electric locomotive No. 27006 *Pandora*. The Longdendale valley could be a hostile place in the depths of winter, but occasionally there were days of superb weather in the summer months when the landscape was transformed into one of scenic splendour.

The new electrified railway in its early years. Here is a Manchester–London train in the charge of a Co-Co electric locomotive passing Rhodeswood Reservoir. Seven of these EMU class Co-Co locomotives were built for passenger duties and fifty-eight EMI class Bo-Bo locomotives were provided for mixed traffic, including the coal trains. Many of the locomotives carried names derived from Greek mythology.

CHAPTER THREE

RAILS IN THE PEAK DISTRICT

The southern Pennines end in the peaks of Derbyshire to reveal a tumbled mass of hills and deep-cleft valleys which stretches out towards the Midland Plain. Here, the dales throw limestone crags into bold relief. There is a beauty in the soft greens of the countryside, with its prolific vegetation watered by streams and rivers of astonishing clarity, on whose banks are stone-built villages, so typical of the county.

This is the territory of the Midland Railway, whose crimson-liveried trains were a familiar part of the scene for many years. It was a railway dedicated to the small locomotive. The 4–4–0 for passenger traffic and the inevitable 0–6–0 goods locomotive were regarded as adequate for most eventualities. It was not until the days of the London, Midland and Scottish Railway that the line aspired to a 4–6–0. Towards the end of steam working the route had graduated to the use of 'Britannia' Pacifics and 2–10–0s from the BR stable.

The most popular locomotives to emerge from the Derby works were the Compound 4–4–0s, which were later multiplied by the LMS. These elegant machines were a familiar sight in the area for many years and this portrait would not be complete without them.

A panoramic view awaits the traveller as the train leaves Chinley for the south. In the foreground is a special excursion train hauled by Hughes 2–6–0 mixed-traffic locomotive No. 42823, a product of the Lancashire and Yorkshire Railway locomotive works at Horwich.

Midland Compound 4–4–0 No. 41063, built at Derby, climbs out of Chinley with a Manchester–Sheffield train. The stone walls, which are such a feature of this part of Derbyshire, divide the hillside in the background. The Midland Railway used 4–4–0 locomotives of various classes for most of its express passenger duties. If extra vehicles were added to the train two locomotives would be used in tandem.

An evening train for Derby leaves Chinley village on the climb to Chinley North Junction. Compound 4–4–0 No. 41190 presents a pleasing study as it forges ahead in the spring sunshine. A gradient of 1 in 90 was encountered by southbound trains on leaving the station and the climb continued to Peak Forest.

No. 41190 overtakes a workman returning home after the day's labour. The stone in this part of Derbyshire is gritstone which has led this area to be called the 'Dark Peak'. This was the result of the weathering properties of the rock, which assumed a dark colour after several years of exposure to the elements.

This is a former War Department locomotive, one of a class of 732 taken into British Railways stock after the Second World War. No. 90449 has a 2–8–0 wheel arrangement. The picture affords a close-up of typical British coal wagons fitted only with handbrakes.

A Chinley to Buxton train leaves behind Fowler 2–6–4T No. 42315, an early member of a class which eventually totalled 124 locomotives. The train has been strengthened to seven vehicles for Saturday traffic.

No. 40550, a rebuilt Johnson 4–4–0 of Midland ancestry, passes Chinley North Junction with a Manchester–Sheffield train in September 1951. The Stanier-designed rolling stock sports both the LMS and the new BR liveries.

Midland Compound 4–4–0 No. 41150 negotiates Chinley North Junction with a train from Sheffield. This was one of a batch built by the LMS. The train has just traversed the Hope Valley line, which runs by way of Edale and Hathersage through some of Derbyshire's rich pastureland. There are two tunnels on the route, Totley (3 miles 950 yd) and Cowburn (2 miles 182 yd).

Springtime in the Derbyshire dales, with their patchwork of gritstone walls and pasture. A train of coal empties approaches Cowburn Tunnel as it heads east from Chinley. At the rear is a familiar brake van of LMS design which helped to control trains on down grades.

A mineral train approaches Chinley from the south with Fowler 0–6–0 No. 44565, an LMS version of the Midland design. The upper quadrant signal has replaced the older type of Midland lower quadrant as seen in the background.

A bird's-eye view of Headstones Viaduct in the limestone country of Monsal Dale is the epitome of much of Derbyshire's landscape. In this tranquil scene a Midland 3F 0–6–0 crosses the River Derwent in high summer.

A Manchester–London express hauled by a 'Jubilee' class locomotive heads south to Derby and London St Pancras through Monsal Dale in Derbyshire. The viaduct of 1861 is 300 ft long and has five stone arches which carry the railway 40 ft above the River Wye. This section of the former Midland Railway has now been closed to traffic. With the demise of the Midland and Great Central routes from Manchester to London, traffic is now concentrated on the former LNWR line to Euston.

CHAPTER FOUR

WANDERINGS IN HAMPSHIRE AND DORSET

The journey between London and Bournemouth takes on a new interest as the train enters Hampshire. After Basingstoke the line to the West of England leaves the Bournemouth route at Worting Junction, where the design of the layout, with its flyover, enables traffic to take it at 50 mph. From here onwards, the train travels by way of the cathedral city of Winchester and the city and port of Southampton.

Most of Hampshire is situated on the central chalk plateau, from where the River Test, one of the finest trout streams in Britain, emerges and flows down to the sea at Spithead. Here in the lush meadowland is the true countryside of England, where the air is heavy with the scent of meadowsweet and cattle graze contentedly on the willow-lined pastures.

After Southampton the train heads for Redbridge, where the line to Salisbury branches off to the right. At the same moment a glimpse is provided of the Solent as the River Test runs into the sea.

One of the delights of the Hampshire landscape is the New Forest, which the railway traverses by way of Brockenhurst. Set aside by the Norman kings as a hunting reserve, it has remained in its natural state with grazing rights for commoners to this day. The approach to the seaside resort of Bournemouth is marked by the many pine trees which are a feature of the heathland in this area.

On a hot summer day, BR Pacific No. 70009 *Alfred the Great* brings the Down 'Bournemouth Belle' Pullman over Redbridge Causeway near Southampton, where the River Test enters the Solent.

The Up 'Bournemouth Belle' approaches Bournemouth Central in the summer of 1951. Newly built 'Britannia' class Pacific No. 70009 *Alfred the Great* is in charge. After calling at Bournemouth, the train only stopped at Southampton on its journey to London Waterloo.

Low tide at Redbridge Causeway, as 'West Country' Pacific No. 34019 *Bideford* heads for Bournemouth with a train from Waterloo. These Bulleid Pacifics were built between 1945 and 1950. Some were named after towns and resorts in the west of England ('West Country' class). Others were named after personalities of the Royal Air Force, together with the aircraft, squadrons and RAF stations operating and taking part in the Battle of Britain ('Battle of Britain' class).

'Lord Nelson' class 4–6–0 No. 30857 *Lord Howe* awaits its turn of duty as the Down 'Bournemouth Belle' leaves Southampton Central behind rebuilt 'Merchant Navy' Pacific No. 35022 *Holland America Line*.

An LSWR B4 class 0–4–0 tank locomotive, used in dock work at Southampton, proceeds on the Up Slow line through Shawford. The chalk and pine trees are familiar sights in Hampshire.

A freight train on the Down Slow line makes steady progress to Southampton behind LSWR 0–6–0 No. 30316 of 1897 vintage. This locomotive illustrates the method of placing the safety valves on the dome, which was a feature of early London and South Western designs.

A local passenger train for Winchester proceeds on the Up Fast line through Shawford. LSWR class M7 0–4–4T No. 30378 with appropriate stock is observed in its natural habitat of the Hampshire countryside. Between 1896 and 1911 105 of these locomotives were built, and all but two were still running in 1954.

The pleasant surroundings of Shawford frame a Waterloo–Bournemouth train as it heads for the south coast. The locomotive is 'West Country' class 4–6–2 No. 34095 *Brentnor*.

A Down Bournemouth train approaches the New Forest near Beaulieu Road, hauled by LSWR T9 class 4–4–0 No. 30730. The area is rich in sandy soil and conifers, with large expanses of heather-covered common populated by wild ponies.

A Waterloo–Bournemouth train passes Battledown Junction after the climb out of Basingstoke. The locomotive is 'West Country' class No. 34093 *Saunton*. Sixty-six of these locomotives were built between 1945 and 1950.

No. 30850 *Lord Nelson*, doyen of the class, enters the New Forest on its way to Brockenhurst with a Southampton to Bournemouth train. These four-cylinder 4–6–0s of Maunsell design were introduced between 1926 and 1929. A later modification was the use of double blastpipes with wide-diameter chimney as illustrated.

Express freight locomotive No. 30498 passes Worting Junction south of Basingstoke with a train for the West Country. The locomotive was built at Eastleigh in 1920 by the London and South Western Railway.

A 'Schools' class 4–4–0 locomotive in charge of the 'Cunarder', a Waterloo–Southampton boat train with Pullman accommodation. This train ran direct into the ocean terminal at Southampton Docks. This facility was later withdrawn with the decline in ocean travel.

No. 30850 *Lord Nelson* approaches Battledown flyover with a Salisbury to Waterloo train. This locomotive is now in the national collection. The 'Lord Nelson' class comprised sixteen locomotives. No. 30859 had 6 ft 3 in driving wheels, as against 6 ft 7 in for the rest of the class. No. 30860 also had a slightly longer boiler. When new in the twenties, they were used on the Dover boat trains, but in the period towards the end of their lives they were concentrated on the Bournemouth and Salisbury lines.

A Down stopping train passes Worting Junction in the heart of good grazing country. It is hauled on a summer evening by No. 31612, a Maunsell 2–6–0 of class U, with 6 ft driving wheels.

This picture affords a good view of the junction, with the West Country lines passing under the flyover. A Bournemouth–Waterloo train, in the charge of rebuilt Pacific No. 35010 *Blue Star*, prepares for the descent to Basingstoke.

A Hayling Island to Havant train crosses the Langstone harbour bridge at high tide. 'Terrier' class 0–6–0T No. 32661 of LBSCR vintage survived into the 1950s – it was built at Brighton in the 1870s.

'Terrier' class 0–6–0 No. 32655 poses for the camera on a summer day at Hayling Island terminus. This class numbered fifty engines which were built between 1872 and 1880 by the London, Brighton and South Coast Railway, many surviving to be taken over by British Railways in 1948.

Class N15X No. 32329 *Stephenson*, here seen at Southampton, was originally a 4–6–4 tank locomotive of the London, Brighton and South Coast Railway. After electrification of the Brighton line it was rebuilt, in company with six others of the class, as a 4–6–0 tender locomotive for use on other routes.

The Down Ilfracombe portion of the 'Devon Belle' leaving Cowley Bridge Junction north of Exeter. The tracks to the right are the Great Western main line to Taunton and Bristol. Southern trains from London Waterloo reached Exeter and the Devon resorts via the diversion from the Bournemouth line at Worting Junction.

'West Country' class No. 34003 *Plymouth* approaches Cowley Bridge Junction near Exeter with the Plymouth portion of the Up 'Devon Belle' Pullman. At Exeter Central these cars would be attached to the main portion of the train from Ilfracombe.

The Ilfracombe portion of the Up 'Devon Belle', complete with observation car, approaches Cowley Bridge Junction behind 'West Country' Pacific No. 34005 *Barnstaple*. The locomotive is painted in Southern malachite green livery but sports the new British Railways number.

CHAPTER FIVE
EAST COAST SHOWCASE

'King's Cross for Scotland' was one of the slogans put out by the London and North Eastern Railway in a bid to capture Anglo-Scottish traffic in the 1930s. It endeavoured to publicize the services of the day, with the emphasis on the 'Flying Scotsman', which had left the terminus at 10 a.m. every weekday since 1862.

The East Coast route had the highest number of Pacific locomotives on the BR network due, in large measure, to the introduction of this type by the LNER authorities under Sir Nigel Gresley. Further Pacifics were designed by Edward Thompson and A.H. Peppercorn and entered traffic in the later 1940s.

Three-figure speeds have been recorded from time to time in the course of normal duties, particularly in the 1930s. On 3 July 1938, the A4 streamlined Pacific No. 4468 *Mallard* achieved a world speed record for a steam locomotive of 126 mph on special braking trials.

From the publicity angle, the route has had a good selection of named expresses over the years, and this continued until the end of steam working. The most spectacular of these was no doubt the streamlined 'Coronation' express of 1937, adorned in two shades of blue with stainless steel trim and complete with 'beaver tail' observation car, which made the London–Edinburgh run in six hours.

The 'Capitals Limited' emerging from Hadley Wood South Tunnel, Hertfordshire, in 1950. This train ran non-stop between the English and Scottish capitals during the summer. In 1953 it was renamed 'The Elizabethan' in honour of Queen Elizabeth II. The locomotive is A4 Pacific No. 60009 *Union of South Africa*, now privately preserved.

This is the famous 'Scotch Goods', introduced by the LNER in the 1930s. Fully fitted with vacuum brakes, it ran at a brisk pace from London King's Cross to Scotland. V2 No. 60929 was one of a class regularly used on this service; here it is climbing to Potter's Bar in Hertfordshire.

A Cambridge to London train on the Ganwick Curve in Hertfordshire, between Hadley North and Potter's Bar tunnels. The locomotive is class B2 4–6–0 No. 61671 *Royal Sovereign*, which was used on royal duties as occasion demanded. The class B2 was a rebuild by Edward Thompson of a Gresley B17 4–6–0 from a three-cylinder to a two-cylinder machine.

A King's Cross to Cambridge train approaches Hadley Wood South Tunnel hauled by 'Sandringham' class B17 4–6–0 No. 61637 *Ford Castle*. At the time of the photograph in 1950, the quadrupled main line in this location was reduced to two at a point behind the photographer. This continued to the northern end of Potter's Bar station, where four tracks resumed. This was something of a bottleneck on this heavily used section of line. Subsequently, a four-track layout was introduced in the mid-1950s, which involved the building of three new tunnels in the localities of Hadley Wood and Potter's Bar.

During Sunday engineering operations on the main line, trains were often diverted via Lincoln, which had been the original route to Scotland. On such a day, A4 No. 60021 *Wild Swan* passes Saxilby in Lincolnshire with a train from King's Cross to Newcastle.

Peppercorn A1 Pacific No. 60157 *North Eastern* nears Saxilby with a diverted Sunday, King's Cross–Edinburgh train. This train was the equivalent of the weekday 'Flying Scotsman'. The 'Scotsman' was one of the few named trains to continue running during the Second World War, but on a slower schedule.

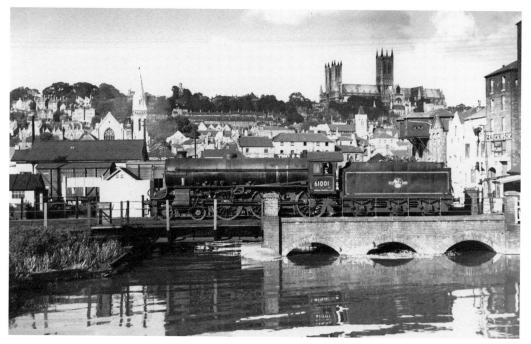

A Lincolnshire townscape. The city of Lincoln provides a backcloth to this study of B1 4–6–0 No. 61001 *Eland*, with the cathedral standing aloft on the skyline. This particular locomotive was second in a class of 410. Designed by Edward Thompson at Doncaster, they were built between 1942 and 1950.

The doyen of the V2 class, No. 60800 *Green Arrow*, in the Lincolnshire countryside south of Grantham on the climb to Stoke Summit. This locomotive is now in the national collection. *Green Arrow* was the first of the V2 class 2–6–2 mixed-traffic locomotives. When new in 1938, it frequently hauled a fast freight service from London King's Cross to Scotland which ran under the Green Arrow motif.

Peppercorn A1 Pacific No. 60118 *Archibald Sturrock* nears Bawtry with the Up 'White Rose', which connected Leeds with London King's Cross. This design appeared in 1948 after nationalization and was developed by A.H. Peppercorn. In all, forty-nine locomotives were built. They were a most successful addition to the Pacific fleet and served the Eastern Region well until the demise of steam.

The Nottinghamshire countryside near Retford is the setting for this view of the Down 'Talisman' which made the London–Edinburgh run in six hours forty minutes. The locomotive is No. 60125 *Scottish Union*, designed by A.H. Peppercorn and built at Doncaster in 1949.

A Leeds to King's Cross express approaches Retford from the north behind Gresley A3 Pacific No. 60108 *Gay Crusader*, newly fitted with double chimney. This particular location was used by the London and North Eastern Railway for official photographs of the new streamlined trains of the 1930s.

In the heart of the Nottinghamshire countryside the hay has been gathered as A1 Pacific No. 60134 *Foxhunter* leaves Askham Tunnel and makes a rapid descent to Retford with a train for Leeds.

In early spring, Gresley A3 Pacific No. 60091 *Captain Cuttle* climbs to Askham Summit with a relief train for London King's Cross. All except five of the seventy-nine locomotives were appropriately named after famous racehorses. The class was built at Doncaster works to the design of Sir Nigel Gresley. The original locomotive *Great Northern* was drastically rebuilt by Edward Thompson in September 1945, to the disdain of Gresley enthusiasts.

This is the Sunday balancing turn of engines which worked the non-stop 'Elizabethan' on weekdays between the two capitals. Here is A4 Pacific No. 60012 *Commonwealth of Australia* passing Gamston box. This locomotive was built at Doncaster in 1937 and was one of five that were allocated to the streamlined 'Coronation' express of that year, which made the journey between the English and Scottish capitals in six hours, including stops at York and Darlington.

The delights of early summer enhance this view of the countryside at Gamston, south of Retford, as the Up 'Tees-Tyne Pullman' proceeds in haste behind A4 Pacific No. 60007 *Sir Nigel Gresley*, named after its designer.

Springtime in Nottinghamshire. A Leeds to King's Cross express climbs past Eaton Wood in the charge of A4 Pacific No. 60013 *Dominion of New Zealand*, built at Doncaster in 1937. The locomotive was fitted with one of the distinctive deep-toned chime whistles of the New Zealand railways.

Possibly the best-known locomotive on the East Coast route. Here, A3 Pacific No. 60103 *Flying Scotsman*, which made the first non-stop run from London to Edinburgh in 1928 with the train of that name, is seen at Grove Road, Retford. Corridor tenders were introduced to enable crews to change over at a halfway point on the journey without stopping the train.

The 'Harrogate Sunday Pullman' emerges from Askham Tunnel, south of Retford, behind A3 Pacific No. 60108 *Gay Crusader*, fitted with a double chimney. This was a popular service introduced by the London and North Eastern Railway in the late 1920s. On the Pullman services, of which there were several, meals were served at every seat. The livery for the cars was cream and umber, while many vehicles carried individual feminine names.

A1 Pacific No. 60147 *North Eastern* is seen in early spring south of Retford with a train for King's Cross. The locomotive is fitted with one of the original stovepipe chimneys.

V2 class 2–6–2 No. 60854 proceeds south with a Leeds to King's Cross express. There were 183 members of this class, introduced in 1936 to the design of Sir Nigel Gresley.

V2 No. 60870 sweeps down from Askham Summit with a King's Cross–Newcastle train. Sheep graze as the train passes Gamston signal-box. This countryside is typical of the eastern counties and of the east coast in general.

An A3 Pacific in full cry. A train to London is seen near Eaton Crossing hauled by No. 60088 *Book Law*, as hay has been safely gathered in the background. No. 60088 was built at Doncaster in 1930 and was withdrawn from service in 1963.

A4 Pacific No. 60033 *Seagull* descends from Askham Tunnel to Retford with a train for Leeds. This locomotive was one of four which received a double chimney when new in 1938, but it was not until the mid-fifties that all the class were so fitted.

No. 60009 *Union of South Africa* hurries south with the Up 'Elizabethan' in the summer of 1955. The journey between the two capitals was accomplished in six hours forty-five minutes nonstop. This locomotive, which was based at Edinburgh for most of its life, survived into preservation.

CHAPTER SIX

MIXED TRAFFIC IN RURAL CHESHIRE AND DERBYSHIRE

Secondary routes and country branch lines are featured in this pictorial survey of Cheshire and Derbyshire. Many of the lines in the area were jointly owned by the Great Central and Midland companies, whose locomotives and rolling stock were to be seen during most of the steam age. At New Mills in Derbyshire, the joint line connected with the Midland Railway from Chinley, and this gave access to Sheffield, Derby, Nottingham, Leicester and London.

There was a substantial amount of freight traffic on the route which was Midland orientated. Part of the route follows that of the Peak Forest Canal for some miles, while at Marple is the superb canal aqueduct of 1808 across the River Goyt, together with the railway viaduct of 1865 which is built alongside. Also of note is the Reddish Viaduct of 1875, which carries the line over the River Tame.

Scenes on the Cheshire Lines Railway depict traffic on the Manchester–Liverpool and Manchester–Wigan lines. It will be noted that many Great Central locomotives were provided for these services almost to the end of steam operations, the Cheshire Lines Committee providing much of the rolling stock.

A train from Manchester leaves Hyde for Woodley and all stations to Macclesfield in a severe frost. The locomotive is a Great Central 4–4–2 tank, a member of the class which took over from the ageing 2–4–2 variety in the 1940s.

L1 2–6–4T No. 67798 near Woodley with a train for Marple. These Thompson locomotives appeared quite late on the scene, before diesel multiple units began operation. The unusual Midland signal-box controls Apethorn Junction, the line to the right being the eastern extremity of the Cheshire Lines Railway to Godley Junction.

A summer day in north-east Cheshire. J11 0–6–0 No. 64293 of Great Central vintage leaves Hyde with a train for Hayfield in Derbyshire. This locomotive was one of a class of 173, of which fifty were still in service in 1961.

A lazy afternoon in high summer near Woodley, as a J11 0–6–0 No. 64357 drifts by with a pick-up goods. Local coal deliveries were made in this way, most towns having their own siding accommodation. A large proportion of goods traffic at this time was composed of loose-coupled wagons fitted only with handbrakes. Towards the end of the decade, however, a move was made to increase the number of vehicles fitted with vacuum brakes.

A Manchester Central–Sheffield Midland train, composed of early LMS corridor stock, leaves Romiley behind Stanier No. 45264. There were 842 of these versatile mixed-traffic locomotives. This train travelled by way of Chinley and the Hope Valley line.

Class C13 4–4–2 No. 67415 makes the descent to Marple after leaving Romiley with a train for Hayfield. The last of the class was withdrawn in 1960. These locomotives were the logical successors to the 2–4–2 tank locomotives designed by Parker in the 1890s and were built at Gorton, Manchester.

A most extraordinary special train from the Eastern Counties approaches Romiley hauled by Great Central 4–4–0 No. 62663 *Prince Albert* and Great Northern Ivatt 4–4–2 No. 251, the latter being allowed out from the national collection. The Peak Forest Canal is in the background. The occasion was a works outing for staff of the Northern Rubber Company, from Retford to Liverpool, by courtesy of Mr Alan Peglar, who was later instrumental in saving No. 4472 *Flying Scotsman* for posterity.

A loose-coupled freight climbs towards Romiley behind Fowler 0–8–0 No. 49650, one of 175 built between 1929 and 1932. Pastoral scenes such as this are the epitome of the English countryside. On a day in early spring, cattle graze undisturbed as the locomotive works hard on the adverse gradient.

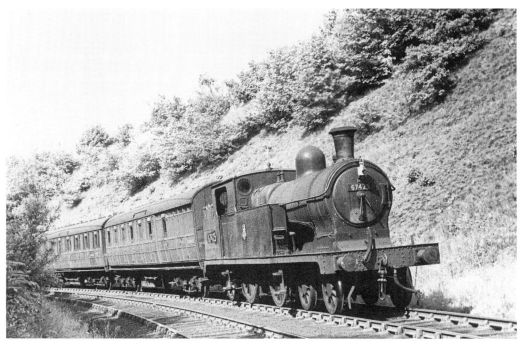

A Manchester–Macclesfield train leaves Marple Wharf Junction and makes a tortuous passage to Rose Hill station behind C13 No. 67425. Until the late 1930s these trains were composed of Great Central six-wheeled stock.

C13 No 67401 approaches Marple Wharf Junction with a train from Macclesfield. The untamed countryside was no doubt a haven for wildlife. In adverse weather during the winter months the Macclesfield line was subject to blockage by snow from time to time. This line now terminates at Marple Rose Hill, the line to Macclesfield having been lifted and converted into a public footpath for use by ramblers and local residents.

LNWR 0–8–0 No. 49093 makes a spirited start as it recovers from a signal check at Marple Wharf Junction with a train of coal from Yorkshire. This particular locomotive was shedded at Belle Vue in Manchester. In 1955, when this photograph was taken, 275 of the class were still in service.

On the main line in early spring 1951 a War Department 2–8–0 freight locomotive toils up the bank from Marple with a train for Manchester. Midland signals poised aloft herald a clear road ahead.

LNWR 0–8–0 No. 49451 runs past Marple Wharf Junction signal-box with a train of coal empties. This locomotive was one of the last of the class to be built at Crewe in 1922.

An interesting view of Marple Viaduct, which spans the Goyt valley. The prolific vegetation is typical of this part of Cheshire. On the viaduct is Midland Compound 4–4–0 No. 1000 on a special working to Gorton locomotive works, shortly after being restored for the national collection.

Great Central 4–6–2 passenger tank locomotive No. 69823 on a running-in turn to Marple, after having attention at Gorton works, where it had been built. These locomotives were not employed on the Manchester suburban services in the course of normal duties.

Adjacent to the railway viaduct is the canal aqueduct, built between 1802 and 1808, which carries the Peak Forest Canal over the Goyt valley. Here, Ivatt 2–6–0 No. 46497 is seen on a passenger working from Chinley to Manchester.

This delightful cameo presents a double portrait (are they brothers?) as J10 0–6–0 No. 65187 of Manchester, Sheffield and Lincolnshire design trundles along through Strines in what is now the High Peak of Derbyshire.

Class 5 4–6–0 No. 44803, in early BR livery, emerges from Marple North Tunnel and passes a superb Midland double-arm signal. In the early 1950s, the signalling system still had many fine pre-grouping specimens.

A Hughes 2–6–0 of a type built at Horwich between 1926 and 1932 descends from the Peak District and approaches Strines with a train of coal. Strines is situated in the foothills of Derbyshire. Gritstone is prevalent in the area. Indeed, many buildings are made out of the local stone and neighbouring New Mills is rich in that respect.

The midday train for Derby enters the sylvan glades of Marple as it departs behind Midland Compound 4–4–0 No. 41118. This picture could only be secured at a certain time of day in the height of summer due to the prolific foliage which otherwise cast dense shadows.

A Manchester–Nottingham train climbs towards the Peak District behind 'Jubilee' class 4–6–0 No. 45667 *Jellicoe*. The LMS rolling stock features early and later designs. It will be noticed that the lush countryside of Marple has given way to a bleaker type of landscape. This change is apparent as the railway approaches Strines.

The Midland and Great Central Joint Line had a branch from Romiley to Ashburys, where it joined the GC into Manchester. The superb viaduct in Reddish Vale provides the background for this glimpse of wildlife in the unspoilt countryside.

Fowler 0–8–0 No. 49509, built at Derby in 1929, proceeds towards Strines with a pick-up goods. This was one of the first examples of a class which numbered 175. It is interesting to compare this LMS-built locomotive with its earlier LNWR counterpart at the bottom of p. 68.

A Manchester–Marple local train climbs out of Reddish behind C13 No. 67424, under the surveillance of a fine Midland double-arm signal. This line deviated from Romiley Junction and ran by way of Bredbury, Reddish and Belle Vue to link up with the GC.

This is one of the earlier series of 'Directors' built in 1913 at work on a Manchester–Liverpool local train near Glazebrook. The locomotive is No. 62655 *The Earl of Kerry*. The Cheshire Plain presented an easy passage between Manchester and Liverpool, so that trains were able to accomplish the journey of 34 miles in forty minutes, with one stop at Warrington.

A Manchester–Wigan train crosses the Cheshire Plain at Glazebrook. This is rather featureless agricultural countryside. The locomotive is a J10 of the former GCR. There were 124 locomotives in this class built between 1892 and 1902. First examples for the Manchester, Sheffield and Lincolnshire Railway were later absorbed into the Great Central stock. Five survived at the close of 1959.

GC 'Director' class 4–4–0 No. 62665 *Mons* leaves Ashley on the former Cheshire Lines Railway with a train for Chester. The Cheshire Lines Committee had no locomotive stock, motive power being provided by British Railways and its predecessors.

J39 0–6–0 mixed-traffic locomotive No. 64717 leaves Ashley with a coal train. These locomotives were designed by Sir Nigel Gresley, this particular example being one of the first of the class to appear in 1926.

Great Central 'Director' class 4–4–0 No. 62669 *Ypres* leaves Ashley with a Chester train. The tall distant signal was typical of Cheshire Lines design. In their heyday these locomotives worked throughout on the Manchester–London expresses.

J10 No. 65173 makes a spirited exit from Glazebrook as it proceeds to Wigan with a local train from Manchester Central. The lower quadrant signal is of Cheshire Lines origin.

CHAPTER SEVEN

EVOCATIVE SCENES IN BERKSHIRE AND DEVON

The Great Western was one or Britain's oldest railways, with its own traditions of service and punctuality. Its main-line route to the counties of Devon and Cornwall gave it the name of the Holiday Line, and many generations were familiar with its Brunswick green engines and chocolate and cream rolling stock. It was the most standardized railway in the British Isles, retaining its identity in the 'grouping' of the railways in 1923. The locomotive and carriage works were at Swindon in Wiltshire.

The locomotives had their own individual style of tapered boiler with brass conical safety valve covering and copper-capped chimney. The Great Western was the line of the 4–6–0 tender locomotive, and several classes evolved with various sizes of boiler and driving wheels for the differing tasks of haulage. Although the company built Britain's first Pacific locomotive, the 4–6–2 wheel arrangement was not perpetuated.

The traveller to the West of England is rewarded by the sight of the River Exe Estuary shortly after leaving Exeter. Here, at low tide, wading birds are in profusion in the mirrored sands of the coastline. At Dawlish and Teignmouth passengers have splendid views of the sea as the train runs by the red sandstone cliffs. Finally, the train climbs over Dartmoor before arriving at Plymouth, famous for its naval and historical associations.

Sonning Cutting in Berkshire, a tranquil and supreme setting on the outskirts of Reading. In high summer the Up 'Torbay Express' drifts serenely towards London in the charge of No. 4085 *Berkeley Castle*.

The Up 'Royal Duchy', captured in the evening light, makes a spirited passage through Sonning Cutting. The train is the 11 a.m. Penzance to London, hauled by No. 6018 *King Henry VI*.

The evening light illuminates No. 5090 *Neath Abbey* of the 'Castle' class as it eases up for the Reading stop with a train for Worcester. The 'Castle' class was a beautifully proportioned express locomotive and was a classic in its own right.

No. 5035 *Coity Castle* pilots a sister engine (unrecorded) on a Paddington–Penzance express in 1957. Double-headed trains were not a feature on this line, but I recorded several on this visit. The immaculate condition of the locomotives should be noted.

Churchward two-cylinder 2–8–0 freight locomotive No. 2824 negotiates Sonning Cutting with a mixed goods on the Up Slow line. This was one of the original engines built between 1903 and 1919.

Collett 2–6–2T locomotive No. 6129 passes Sonning with a Reading to Paddington train. The 5 ft 8 in driving wheels ensured rapid acceleration from stops. A red livery was in use for suburban rolling stock at this time in the mid-1950s.

The Down 'Torbay Express,' hauled by a 'Castle' class locomotive (unrecorded), prepares for the next stop at Reading. The locomotive would work throughout to Kingswear in Devon via Bristol, Exeter, Torquay and Paignton.

On a summer evening the Wallingford branch train, hauled by 0–4–2T No. 1436, proceeds along the Up Slow line and is overtaken by a Worcester–Paddington express hauled by No. 5024 *Carew Castle*.

The Down 'Cornish Riviera Express' passes Cowley Bridge Junction near Exeter in 1951 hauled by No. 6023 *King Edward II* in experimental light blue livery. This colour was abandoned in favour of dark green.

No. 5024 *Carew Castle* leaves Kingskerswell on the Torbay branch with a train from Dartmouth to Exeter. The line was used to capacity on summer Saturdays when holidays were at their peak.

No. 6019 *King Henry V*, with double chimney, brings a Paddington–Plymouth train through Dawlish Warren. The fitting of twin blastpipes and double chimney was a modification to the design after the Second World War to enable the locomotive to exploit the poorer grades of coal then coming into use.

The Up 'Torbay Express' approaches Dawlish Warren in south Devon, which is noted for its red sandstone cliffs. Here the railway runs along the coast for several miles to the delight of travellers. In severe winters, however, the sea can play havoc with the line, sometimes causing flooding. The locomotive is No. 5062 *Earl of Shaftesbury*.

The countryside embraces the sea in this view of the Devon coastline. Here, a Great Western 2–8–0 with a train carrying stone is seen against the light in this evocative setting.

Clear road ahead as the Up 'Cornish Riviera Express' runs along the coast near Teignmouth to the next stop at Exeter. The walls, made of local stone, blend perfectly with the surroundings.

High tide, as the Up 'Torbay Express', hauled by a locomotive of the 'Castle' class, passes Teignmouth on its sprint to Exeter and London. The locomotive for this prestige working was usually a member of the 'Castle' class, but locomotives of the 'King' class were also used occasionally.

The Down 'Torbay Express' emerges from the red sandstone portal of Parsons Tunnel, Dawlish, behind No. 5079 *Lysander* in 1958. This is one of the locomotives of the class which were renamed during the war after well-known military aircraft.

The Up 'Torbay Express' runs along the Teign estuary as it approaches Teignmouth behind No. 5080 *Defiant*. The name is another wartime renaming gesture.

High tide is approaching as a 'Castle' class locomotive on the Down 'Cornishman' leaves Teignmouth alongside the Teign estuary. This train came into operation in the summer of 1890 and was the fastest train at that time between London and the West of England.

The Up 'Cornish Riviera Express', hauled by No. 6004 *King George III*, approaches Teignmouth on its run to Paddington in the summer of 1958. This train was invariably worked by one of the 'King' class 4–6–0s based at Old Oak Common (London) or Laira (Plymouth).

CHAPTER EIGHT

TRAINS IN THE HILLS – BEATTOCK AND THE CLYDE VALLEY

In steam days the journey from Carlisle to Glasgow had an air of expectancy. As the train proceeded north via Floriston, views of the Solway Firth presented themselves on the left, before the Scottish border was crossed near Gretna, 399 miles from London. On arrival at Beattock most trains were provided with a banking locomotive to enable them to tackle the formidable 10 mile climb to the summit (1000 ft), partly on a gradient of 1 in 74. The summit signal-box stood in complete isolation in an area of bleak moorland. The line then descended to Elvanfoot and the Clyde valley, an area of outstanding beauty, where the railway accompanied the river on its journey to Glasgow.

In the villages along the line there was the peace and tranquility of a bygone age where, in the sparkling waters of the Clyde, trout rode out the turbulence undisturbed.

On a fine summer evening, 'Britannia' class Pacific No. 70050 *Firth of Clyde* leaves Floriston Woods as it heads for Carlisle with the evening Glasgow–Manchester train. No. 70050 was one of the members of the class allocated to the Scottish Region.

This is an LMS development of the Midland class 2 4–4–0 built at Derby between 1928 and 1932. No. 40614, with an original Midland-pattern chimney, leaves Dumfries with a train for Stranraer.

A special train leaves Dumfries for Glasgow behind Great North of Scotland 4–4–0 No. 49 *Gordon Highlander*, which was an early candidate for preservation. The rear Pullman observation car was originally employed on the Southern's 'Devon Belle' service in the early 1950s.

A train of local coal supplies leaves Beattock behind Caledonian 0–4–4 tank locomotive No. 55260, as workmen on the lineside stop to admire their handiwork. The branch to Moffat on the right was regularly operated by these locomotives.

The Up 'Royal Scot' from Glasgow approaches Beattock station at a lively pace. It is hauled by No. 46254 *City of Stoke on Trent*, with appropriate headboard. In the other direction, the 10 miles to the summit, partly at a gradient of 1 in 74, was one of the most exacting stretches on British Railways.

Stanier class 5 No. 45153, with a fitted freight for the South, approaches Elvanfoot and climbs to the summit at Beattock. For the benefit of northbound trains, a signal-box was positioned at the summit for dealing with banking engines, which would then return to Beattock station at the foot of the incline.

Sitting pretty. A Caledonian 0–6-0 goods locomotive reposes in the siding at Elvanfoot as the crew await their next turn of duty. This engine has acquired a tender from one of the 'Oban' bogies scrapped in the 1930s.

War Department 2–10–0 No. 90767 prepares to resume its journey south as it receives the signal on the freight storage siding at Elvanfoot. These wartime locomotives were built from 1943 onwards, twenty-five surviving to be taken into BR stock in 1948.

The Down 'Royal Scot' sweeps through Elvanfoot on the descent from Beattock in the charge of No. 46225 *Duchess of Gloucester*. The unique pagoda-style signal-box is of Caledonian design. The two Nissen huts had survived from the Second World War.

Summer morning in the Clyde valley as a Caledonian 0–6–0 brings the pick-up goods into Crawford. The rolling countryside in this area is an absolute delight, with the railway, road and the River Clyde making their passage to Glasgow. Many of the stations along the Clyde valley had their own siding accommodation at this time. This facility was withdrawn, together with the local passenger services, when the stations were demolished for the forthcoming electrification of the line which was inaugurated in May 1974.

The Up 'Caledonian' approaches Crawford in the early morning mist behind Stanier Pacific No. 46244 *King George VI*. This train was introduced in 1957 and made the Glasgow–London run in 6 hours 40 minutes with one stop at Carlisle. The 'Duchess' class Pacifics appeared to monopolize this working.

A train of empty coal wagons is hauled south by Stanier class 5 4–6–0 No. 44900, approaching Crawford on the climb to Beattock. This class had 842 engines built by the LMS and BR between 1934 and 1951. There were various subdivisions within the class, providing differences in boiler mountings, etc.

The double-headed evening Glasgow–Manchester train speeds south as sheep graze contentedly in the pastures below. The Scots pine trees are a familiar sight in this area of the Scottish Lowlands between Abington and Crawford.

Stanier Pacific No. 46224 *Princess Alice* forges ahead with the Perth–London express through the Clyde valley to the north of Crawford. This locomotive was built in 1937 and was one of five allocated to the 'Coronation Scot' working.

Pacific No. 46252 *City of Leicester* thunders down the gradient (indicated by the lineside post) between Crawford and Abington with the London–Perth express.

An atmospheric portrait of the Clyde valley in the dramatic evening light showing a class 5 4–6–0 on a fitted freight climbing to Beattock. The valley provides several impressions of mood and atmosphere during tranquil summer evenings.

As shadows fall, the crisp evening air is apparent in this evocative view of a fitted freight on its climb to Beattock Summit. In the stillness of the hour the trail of steam would hang suspended long after the train had gone.

A Glasgow–Manchester train leans into the curve as it proceeds towards Crawford. The locomotive is BR Standard Pacific No. 72001 *Clan Cameron*, built at Crewe in the 1950s. The 'Clan' Pacifics were a small class of ten locomotives and all were based in Scotland where they worked on secondary duties. These locomotives had 6 ft 2 in driving wheels and two outside cylinders.

BR Pacific No. 72003 *Clan Fraser* heads south with a Glasgow Fair holiday express for Blackpool. In the background is the Clyde which can be seen on the approach to Abington.

Stanier Pacific No. 46226 *Duchess of Norfolk* leaves Abington with a relief Glasgow–London express. This locomotive, built at Crewe in 1938, was originally streamlined and painted in maroon and gilt livery.

Pacific No. 46209 *Princess Beatrice*, one of a class of thirteen locomotives, approaches Abington with a London–Perth express. The class included the Turbomotive, which was a variation on the design. These locomotives made a substantial impact on Anglo-Scottish services when introduced in 1933.

A BR class 3 2–6–0 approaches Abington with a mixed goods from the North. No. 77005 was one of a class of twenty engines built in 1954. The Scottish thistle can be seen in abundance on the lineside.

CHAPTER NINE

STEAM FINALE ON THE GLASGOW–ABERDEEN ROUTE

In 1895 the section of railway between Kinnaber Junction and Aberdeen saw the most extraordinary scenes in British railway history, when the rival east and west coast companies, in a fierce bout of racing mania, endeavoured to reach the Granite City from London in the shortest possible time. Kinnaber Junction was the point where the two routes converged for the final stretch into Aberdeen.

It was not until the eleventh hour of steam working, however, that I availed myself, through the kindness of the authorities, of the opportunity to take photographs on this most scenic section of the route. I make no apologies, therefore, for extending this selection into the early 1960s in order to portray this very special scene.

Perhaps the most interesting locomotives to be built for the railway were the six 2–8–2 express locomotives designed by Sir Nigel Gresley, of which the first was the celebrated *Cock o' the North* of 1934. Some of the A4 Pacifics were reprieved to work the 3 hour Glasgow–Aberdeen services before their demise in the mid-1960s, and these are featured in this photographic appreciation.

The 'Grampian Express' from Aberdeen to Glasgow was one of a trio of named trains which served this route and which were entrusted to Pacific haulage in the Indian summer of steam working. The journey was accomplished in 3 hours 30 minutes. Peppercorn A2 Pacific No. 60532 *Blue Peter* is seen on the north-east coast near Stonehaven with this train.

The railway between Aberdeen and Stonehaven was a veritable switchback and Scottish locomotive crews required all their great skills and expertise. A4 Pacific No. 60024 *Kingfisher* on its 3 hour flight between Aberdeen and Glasgow is seen against the backcloth of the North Sea as the train passes Muchalls, 11 miles outside the Granite City.

The evening service from Glasgow to Aberdeen was named the 'St Mungo'. Here is the train on the final stage of the journey, crossing Muchalls Viaduct hauled by A4 Pacific No. 60034 *Lord Faringdon*. These locomotives were allocated to Aberdeen's Ferryhill depot.

No. 60004 *William Whitelaw* passes Cove Bay with a Fridays only train to Edinburgh. The locomotive is on the climb out of Aberdeen and is seen in the mellow light of evening against the expanse of the North Sea. In summertime this coast is idyllic, but in winter it can be a cruel place.

Peppercorn A2 Pacific No. 60527 *Sun Chariot* climbs out of Stonehaven with the 'Grampian' service to Glasgow. The other member of the trio of named expresses on this route was the 'Bon Accord'.

A class V2 2–6–2 on a southbound freight begins the severe climb out of Stonehaven on a hot summer afternoon. The gradient out of Stonehaven was 1 in 90, which entailed hard work for the heavier trains.

A V2 locomotive descends the bank into Stonehaven with a Dundee to Aberdeen train. The Aberdeenshire countryside complements this study of No. 60818.

The severity of the climb out of Stonehaven is shown to advantage in this view taken in the glen of Carron Water. A3 Pacific No. 60100 *Spearmint* is at the head of a train for Edinburgh. This locomotive was based in Scotland all its life and was one of the last survivors of its class being withdrawn in June 1965.

Deep in the glen, A4 Pacific No. 60024 *Kingfisher* climbs the bank out of Stonehaven with the afternoon train for Glasgow. This locomotive was built at Doncaster in 1936 and was one of two which survived until the demise of the class in September 1966. It finished its days at Aberdeen's Ferryhill depot.

Peppercorn A2 Pacific No. 60527 *Sun Chariot* leaves Hilton Junction near Perth with a train from Aberdeen to Glasgow. Most of these locomotives appeared after nationalization, although one, named after the designer, emerged in the final days of the LNER.

A freight train approaches Moncrieff Tunnel outside Perth hauled by Thompson B1 4–6–0 No. 61076. On emerging from the south end of the tunnel the train would take the east coast route at Hilton Junction and proceed in the direction of Edinburgh.

A diesel-assisted freight enters Moncrieff Tunnel near Perth behind North British J37 0–6–0 No. 64591. This locomotive was originally built by the North British Railway in 1919 and survived until October 1964.

A Glasgow train emerges out of the tunnel at Hilton Junction, where the line to Edinburgh diverges to the right. The locomotive is BR Pacific No. 70007 *Coeur de Lion* of the 'Britannia' class.

The approach to Moncrieff Tunnel from the south. War Department 2–8–0 No. 90020 passes Hilton Junction signal-box with a freight from the Edinburgh line.

CHAPTER TEN

LOOSE COUPLINGS

In the course of its history the steam locomotive has fired the imagination of writers, film makers, artists and photographers. In retrospect, the spectacle of smoke and steam provoked an atmosphere of pure theatre, and the station farewells, so beloved of film makers, produced scenes of emotional tenderness and drama. In the precincts of a railway station, express locomotives at rest exuded an aura or presence, the simmering of steam giving the impression of some form of life.

After nearly one hundred and fifty years in use on the railways of this country, it is not surprising that the steam locomotive has aroused the same emotions as the sailing ships of old. The train in full flight provided something of the thrill of the chase, and to pursue this aspect, many miles of travel on the railways of Britain has resulted in this collection of photographs.

In this final selection, in which the photographs are arranged in suitable pairings, the author has indulged in a little nostalgia. They represent special moments in time which have been savoured and recorded by the camera. As we approach the end of the line, so to speak, these pictures conclude the memories and impressions of steam in the countryside, when the railway was at one with nature in what was one of the most interesting decades of the century.

Former Great Eastern 2–4–0 No. 62790, with appropriate rolling stock, nears Haverhill in Suffolk with a train from Marks Tey. This locomotive, built in 1896, remained in service until January 1956. One of the class has been restored for the national collection, most of which is displayed in the National Railway Museum at York.

A3 Pacific No. 60093 *Coronach* emerges from the Mound Tunnel in Prince's Street Gardens, Edinburgh, on its way to the motive power depot at Haymarket.

A4 Pacific No. 60024 *Kingfisher* traverses Prince's Street Gardens on its way to take up duties at Waverley station.

2–4–0 No. 2781 nears Haverhill in the heat of a summer afternoon. This class first appeared in 1891 and one hundred engines were built, several surviving into the 1950s.

Moneymusk station on the Alford branch in Aberdeenshire is the location of this delightful view of Great North of Scotland 4–4–0 No. 49 *Gordon Highlander*, which had been recently restored when the photograph was taken.

In freezing conditions a Manchester–Sheffield local train passes Chinley North Junction in the charge of Compound No. 41114. This is the epitome of steam locomotives battling against the elements.

Under the shadow of Ben Nevis, K4 2–6–0 No. 61995 *Cameron of Lochiel* has just arrived at Fort William shed on its last outing before withdrawal. It was one of six locomotives specially designed for the West Highland line in the 1930s by Sir Nigel Gresley.

The spectacle of picking up water on the move. Two Great Central 'Director' class 4–4–0s, Nos 62662 *Prince of Wales* and 62664 *Princess Mary*, replenish their tanks on Luddendenfoot troughs in Lancashire and Yorkshire Railway territory.

The Britannia tubular bridge in North Wales, which spanned the Menai Strait, was completed to the design of Robert Stephenson in 1850. This linked the mainland to Anglesey, the terminus being at Holyhead with steamer connections. This photograph was secured in the 1950s. However, on 23/24 May 1970 the bridge suffered a disastrous fire and had to be rebuilt.

The Down 'Thames–Clyde Express' passing Dent on the Settle and Carlisle section of the former Midland Railway. 'Britannia' class Pacific No. 70054 *Dornoch Firth* was host to Bishop Eric Treacy, the celebrated railway photographer, who was on the footplate on this occasion.

A special train to view the Britannia Tubular bridge is in the charge of Fowler 2–6–4 tank locomotive No. 42366, which had been built at the Midland works at Derby. Impressive lion sculptures guard the entrance to the bridge.

What was to be the last steam train to run on British Railways surmounts Ais Gill Summit under the shadow of Wild Boar Fell on 11 August 1968. Stanier class 5 4–6–0 Nos 44871 and 44781 pay their last respects. Fortunately public pressure has ensured that steam engines continue to run.

The magic of the Lune valley. A vision of tranquility as seen from the railway.

Here time was of no consequence. After the passage of the 10.15 the air was full of birdsong, as insects hovered in the long grass, and the babbling brook chattered into eternity.

BIBLIOGRAPHY

Batty, Stephen B. *The Woodhead Route*, Ian Allan, 1986.
Casserley, H.C. and Asher L.L. *Locomotives of British Railways*, Spring Books, 1961.
Railway Correspondence and Travel Society *Locomotives of the LNER. Part 2A: Tender Engines Classes A1 to A10*, Railway Correspondence and Travel Society 1973.
Radford, B. *Midland Through The Peak*, Unicorn Books, 1986.